Sister Wendy
on the Art of
SAINTS

Sister Wendy Beckett

Franciscan
MEDIA
Cincinnati, Ohio

Cover and book design by Mark Sullivan. Sister Wendy image © Photoshot.
Cover image *St. Catherine of Alexandria*, attributed to Benevenuto Tisi Garofalo, c. 1515-1530, copyright © National Gallery, London/Art Resource, NY.

LIBRARY OF CONGRESS CATALOGING-IN-PUBLICATION DATA
Beckett, Wendy.
Sister Wendy on the art of saints / Sister Wendy Beckett.
pages cm
Summary: "Imagine going on a tour of a world-class art museum with a talented and insightful curator. But instead of just focusing on the history, technique, and cultural significance of each piece, you have the opportunity to reflect on the spiritual aspects of the works, examining their religious significance and concentrating on the transcendental meaning conveyed by the artist. This is what you'll find in this exquisitely produced book. Sister Wendy writes with the deft hand of one who is formed in spirituality, art, and critical thinking. Her imagery is lush, creating a landscape where the sacred and profane live in comfortable coexistence through the medium of painting. For spiritual seekers and lovers of art, this book will offer a unique journey into the experiential nature of a well-rounded faith"— Provided by publisher.
ISBN 978-1-61636-697-1 (pbk.)
1. Christian saints in art. 2. Christian saints—Meditations. I. Title.
N8079.5.B43 2013
700'.4823—dc23
2013018829

ISBN 978-1-61636-697-1

Published by Franciscan Media
28 W. Liberty St.
Cincinnati, OH 45202
www.FranciscanMedia.org

Printed in the United States.
Printed on acid-free paper.
13 14 15 16 17 5 4 3 2 1

Contents

PICTURE CREDITS

St. John the Baptist Retiring to the Desert, by Giovanni di Paolo, 1454, (Predella Panel from an Altarpiece)
   Copyright © National Gallery, London | Art Resource, NY

Noli me Tangere, by Titian, 1514
   Image courtesy of Wikimedia Commons/the Yorck Project

St. Cecilia, by Pietro da Cortona, c. 1620–1625
   Copyright © National Gallery, London | Art Resource, NY

The Martyrdom of St. Agatha, by Giovanni Battista Tiepolo, 1750
   Staatlich Museen zu Berlin, Gemäldegalerie, Berlin, Germany

St. Dorothy and the Infant Christ, by Francesco di Giorgio, 1460
   Copyright © National Gallery, London | Art Resource, NY

St. George and the Dragon, by Paolo Uccello
   Image courtesy of Wikimedia Commons/the Yorck Project

St. Catherine of Alexandria, attributed to Benevenuto Tisi Garofalo, c. 1515–1530
   Copyright © National Gallery, London | Art Resource, NY

The Vision of St. Helena, by Paolo Veronese, c. 1560–1565
   Copyright © National Gallery, London | Art Resource, NY

St. Jerome in a Rocky Landscape, attributed to Joachim Patinir, c. 1520
   Copyright © National Gallery, London | Art Resource, NY

St. Francis Renounces his Earthly Father, by Sassetta, c. 1437–1444
   Copyright © National Gallery, London | Art Resource, NY

St. Serapion, by Francisco de Zurbarán, 1628
   Image courtesy of Wikimedia Commons/the Yorck Project

St. Thomas Aquinas, by Carlo Crivelli, 1476
   Copyright © National Gallery, London | Art Resource, NY

Bernadette's Embroidery, by Greg Tricker, 2008
   Private collection; image courtesy of Piano Nobile Gallery, London

St. Thérèse of Lisieux, photograph, 1881
   Carmelite Monastery at Lisieux

INTRODUCTION

We are all born and each of us will die: Those are the two certainties of life. In between these certainties God has given us the gift of time so that we may grow into the fullness of what we are meant to be. This fullness is different for each of us, but the ways in which it is achieved are the same.

Since God made us in his own image and we know what that image is through the historical actuality of Jesus, each person's fullness is an attainment of a likeness to our Blessed Lord. When we are as God wants us to be, we will have within us what St. Paul calls "the mind of Christ." We learn this "mind" most of all by prayer, silent prayer, and the wonder of sacramental prayer. We learn it through reading the Scriptures where God reveals himself in his Son, and, complimentary to that, we come close to Our Blessed Lord in the books written by those who have understood the Scriptures.

Yet prayer, worship, and reading are only a part of our day (though, literally speaking, everything is or should be prayer). One of the most neglected truths is that we learn to become like Jesus through the actual process of living. God is giving himself to us all the time; but all too often we do not see it. He gives himself in human relations, in nature, in literature, in music, in art. This book is an attempt to show how he gives himself to us in art.

Artists have an awareness of something greater than themselves, as do most of us. The crucial difference is that they can make this awareness visible. Art draws us out of our own smallness into what one could call a vision for which there are no words. We experience it through the artist's skill, but to reach this experience we have to look very closely at what the artist has done.

In many of the works I have chosen, what the artist puts before us flows from a scriptural narrative or some other aspect of faith. We cannot encompass the liberating power of the vision unless we understand the essential elements of the story. Looking closely and letting the work reveal itself to us is a paradigm of all looking. How are we to seek God if we do not look?

Once we have learned the deep joy of looking at art—which can also be an alarming challenge, when we see things in ourselves that we would rather not see—we are emboldened in our looking at the life in which we are embedded.

One of the verses of Scripture that moves me most deeply is the great cry with which Jesus died on the cross: "It is consummated." He had fulfilled completely the will of his Father. He had never neglected or passed by that holy will, displaying itself in the most ordinary of circumstances.

None of us can come even near this wonder of "consummation." We have missed so much, not out of malice but through sheer ignorance and lack of interest. We do not take enough trouble, to paraphrase St. John Vianney. God was there but we did not see him.

When you look at the pictures in this book, really look, opening your heart to take in what is there before you, you are not only responding to a particular work of art, you are practicing the habit of openness to the beauty of God as he illuminates every moment of your every day. Understood correctly, appreciating and understanding art is a profound form of prayer. It changes us. Or rather, it will change us if we allow the Holy Spirit to utter within us the total yes of Jesus to the Father.

—*Sister Wendy*

St. John the Baptist, first century

St. John the Baptist Retiring to the Desert, 1454, Giovanni di Paolo
The National Gallery, London

St. John the Baptist is unique among the saints. He belongs as much to the Old Testament as he does to the New: He is a prophet, but he is the last of the prophets. His great moment, of course, was when he was called by Jesus to baptize him, and it is naturally that scene artists most often depict. There are some wonderful paintings of John preaching, but it is John standing in the Jordan with Jesus, reverently baptizing him, that is the crucial image. They look so alike: two young men—yet one the Son of God, and the other of whom Jesus said, "among those born of women no one has arisen greater than John the Baptist; yet the least in the kingdom of heaven is greater than he" (Matthew 11:11).

John the Baptist lived in the desert, in conditions of extreme austerity. He wore camel skin with a leather girdle and lived on locusts and wild honey. Giovanni di Paolo is inspired to show us the little John, setting out from his parents' house with its fancy frontage, and leaving all the comforts of home so that he can live alone with God.

It is a very rare depiction of a lovable and even charming John.

He is still in his pretty pink garment, and, like all young adventurers, he carries on his shoulder a stick from which hangs a small bag of provisions. This image suggests that he did not anticipate the full rigors of what would be his vocation. He launched himself upon it with a full heart, and it would be in the years ahead that God would unfold to him the true dimensions of his vocation—just like us, in fact.

We think of holiness as a state of closeness to Jesus. That is the longing of every saint, and of every Christian—to be like Jesus. But for most of his life John was compared to Jesus, and not always to his disadvantage. John fitted much more the pattern of what people think of as sanctity, there in the desert "neither eating nor drinking." Jesus lived among his fellow men and women, a much more ordinary life. He ate and drank, went to parties, blessed children, and had women followers. The Pharisees, who said of John the Baptist "he has a demon," called Jesus "a glutton and a drunkard, a friend of tax collectors and sinners" (Matthew 11:18, 19).

John saw very little, physically, of Jesus, yet surely he was united to him more profoundly than anyone except Our Lady. We can see how pointless it is to compare their lifestyles, and this holds equally for each of us. No one vocation is better than another. The penitential solitary in the desert lost for hours in contemplation may be no closer to God than the busy mother or taxi driver or schoolteacher (fill in your own profession). All God asks is that we respond completely to our own vocation, however ordinary it may seem.

Jesus gloried in the vocation of John. John pondered anxiously over the vocation, the meaning, of Jesus. His was the glory of preparing the way of the Lord, a way he himself was not privileged to travel. We see the fullness of his holiness in his humble acceptance of this.

St. Mary Magdalene, first century

Noli me Tangere, 1514, Titian
The National Gallery, London

Artists have always been attracted to Mary Magdalene. Often they show her in penance, weeping for her sins, for some reason bare to the waist, long hair streaming down her back. Or they show her, beautiful and seductive, holding an alabaster jar of ointment. But this is because they have confused her with two other women in the New Testament: the Mary out of whom Jesus cast seven devils, and the sinful woman who broke a precious alabaster jar of ointment over his feet when he was dining with Simon the Pharisee. This conflation has no historical validity and, moving though these other depictions are, they cannot reveal to us the Magdalene who spoke to Jesus after the Resurrection.

The Gospel of John brings us very close to this woman. Her heart was broken by the death of Jesus, and all she could do to show her love was to prepare his body, wash and clean it, as had not been done after his hurried burial. Her anguish when she finds even this last service is not possible comes across very clearly to us. The tomb is empty: "They have taken away my Lord, and I do not know where they have laid him" (John 20:13).

She means this literally, but many Christians have times when their faith seems dim—they cannot "find" Jesus. They must cling to an intellectual certainty that this absence is not objective; it is only emotionally that for them he seems not present. But for Mary Magdalene, it is fully objective, as she roams the garden on Easter morning, blinded by tears, searching for Jesus.

Whoever searches, finds. Mary Magdalene does indeed find; she meets him, and, as is so often the case with us, she does not recognize him. She thinks he is the gardener, and Titian shows Jesus holding a hoe, which explains her mistake. One of the most moving passages in the whole of Scripture is when the so-called gardener turns to her and says, "Mary." She may not recognize him, but Jesus recognizes her. He is the one who searches, far more than we do.

We know what happens next, how she drops to her knees, lifted in one moment from the depths of sorrow to the heights of joy. (Perhaps death will be like this for us?) She stretches out her arms to him, and Jesus explains that this is his risen body, not to be touched—only to be adored and loved and praised. "*Noli me tangere*," he says, "Do not touch me." So, piercing through her ecstatic joy comes the pain of reality. Like us, she must adore "in spirit and in truth," no longer in body.

You may object that this is a picture of Jesus, rather than of Mary Magdalene, but that is how every saint would choose to be depicted. None of them exists in his or her own right, as it were. All of them take their meaning from the presence of Jesus in their lives.

Mary Magdalene had the privilege, of which she was fully aware, of being contemporary with Jesus. Apart from the New Testament saints, all—including ourselves—can only enter this world through prayer. Remember, though, that not everybody who knew Our Lord shared his life. Think of the Pharisees and his other enemies. Our manner of closeness, which depends wholly on faith, can be as transformative for us as physical closeness to Jesus was for Mary Magdalene and the apostles.

If we were to demand a visual representation of what it means to be a saint, this painting might be a good answer. Mary is on her knees looking up to Jesus, absorbed in him, and he holds out a hand in blessing. This is precisely what happens for us, when we pray.

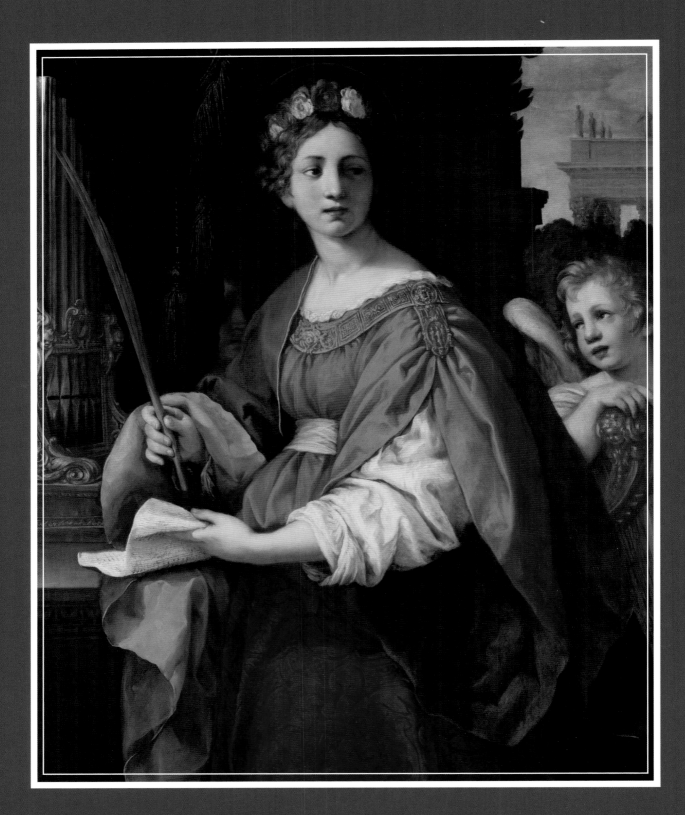

St. Cecilia, second to third century

St. Cecilia, 1620–1625, Pietro da Cortona
The National Gallery, London

There are quite a few virgin martyrs from the first centuries, and artists, throwing probability loftily aside, depict all of them as young and beautiful. So that we can distinguish one from another, each has in the course of time acquired an emblem or symbol. These attributes are usually taken from the account of their martyrdom: for example, St. Catherine has the wheel that was supposed to tear her to pieces, St. Apollonia has the forceps that violently drew out all her teeth, St. Margaret has the dragon that swallowed her (until she forced her way out with a crucifix), St. Barbara has the tower in which she was imprisoned. St. Cecilia is a little different. She is the patron saint of music and her emblem is the portable organ, as well as whatever other musical instruments strike the artist's fancy.

Pietro da Cortona shows St. Cecilia holding the palm of martyrdom in one hand, while on her knee she holds pages of manuscript: hymns? Behind her, within easy reach, on the left as we look at the picture, is her organ, while on the right an angel looks soulfully up at her, holding a harp. Yet music had nothing to do with her death, and in fact, it is not easy to pinpoint the factors that have so intimately linked her name with music.

Cecilia was a young woman of high patrician birth. The site of her ancestral home is believed to be underneath the ancient church of St. Cecilia in Trastevere. As was inevitable with highborn ladies of the time, she was married off against her will, but here she had a great stroke of good fortune.

Cecilia's bridegroom, a pagan called Valerius, must have been an exceptional young man. When she explained to him her desire to live a life of virginity for the sake of Christ, he accepted her decision. The legend tells us that during the marriage ceremonies she sang to God in her heart, and it may be from this spiritual singing that the belief arose that she was especially musical. Valerius and his brother Tiburtius were so impressed by the strength of her faith that they too became Christians and were martyred even before the judges came for Cecilia.

The story then becomes rather confused, with one account holding that she was suffocated to death by boiling steam in her private bathroom, another that she was merely beheaded. How she died seems much less important than how she lived, and whatever the literal truth of her story, the impression left on Christian Rome was that she was one who expressed her love of God through her love of music.

This is more important than it might seem. There appears to be in human nature a fear of pleasure, and the saints are so often shown as those who embrace eagerly penance and mortification. But God comes to us through all the beauty of the world, just as much as in its pain. God is there in sunlight and in summer as much as in storms and in winter. Some people, some saints, have tormented themselves over such things as their love for literature, like St. Jerome, or their loathing of cheese, like St. Margaret Mary Alacoque. But God is very present in literature, and God is very present in a physical incapacity to digest a food. We need constantly to remind ourselves of God's all-pervading presence, how God wants to come to us at every angle, at every moment, and how we are missing God because we are inattentive or narrow-minded.

It is hard not to be aware of God's divine presence in music. It can lift us out of the limitations of our selfishness, rather in the way that prayer does. If some painting is visual prayer, then music can be aural prayer.

When we respond to the psalms, and "sing and make music to the Lord," we are in communion with St. Cecilia.

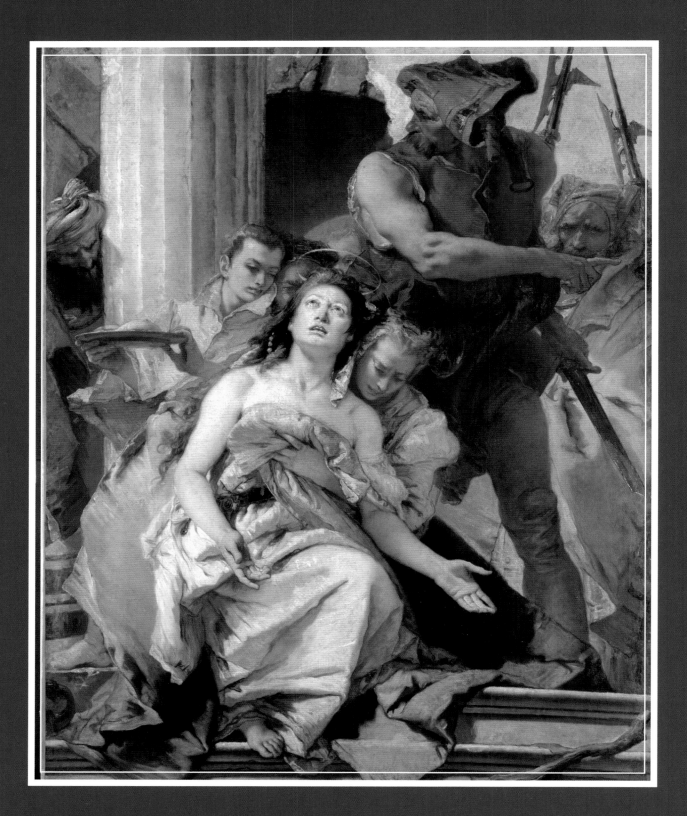

St. Agatha, died c. 250

The Martyrdom of St. Agatha, 1750, Giovanni Battista Tiepolo
Staatliche Museen zu Berlin, Gemäldegalerie, Berlin

When I was about ten, my mother bought the full set of Butler's *Lives of the Saints*. I can see them now, green and gold, in the glass cabinet. I was thrilled at the thought of all these large, holy books to read, but I confess, with shame, that I never got further than the first volume. It was St. Agatha who stopped me in my eager tracks.

For one just beginning to understand that one passed from childhood into, eventually, womanhood, reading what was done to Agatha aroused a great wave of fear, indignation, and grief. Because she would not sacrifice to the pagan gods, the Roman authorities cut off her breasts and she bled to death. I could not bear it, yet bearing what happens in life is the way to God.

I sorrowed for a long time over poor, mutilated St. Agatha, and the terrible choices that some people are evidently asked to make. Even if I foolishly read no more of Butler's *Lives*, at least I had read enough to make me realize my own softness and weakness, and how very much I had need of the support of prayer.

During that sorrowing time, I wish I had seen Tiepolo's painting of St. Agatha in her martyrdom. He disguises none of the pain or horror, but he shows with extraordinary power what this dying girl did with that pain.

In the painting she is already almost bloodless. Her face, deathly white, is in striking contrast to the two healthy faces that press in on either side. Neither seems hostile. The page boy is bearing away the two pathetic mounds of flesh that are her breasts. The pagan priestess helps hold the cloth to her wounds. Both look vaguely interested, but essentially unconcerned. The executioner looms savagely over her, and a prurient bystander peeks at the plate. Agatha is dying without any obvious divine support. She holds out her hands with her fading strength, and lifts her face to heaven, tear-stained with red-rimmed eyes.

Nothing in art to me surpasses that dying look. It always reminds me of that line from the book of Job in the Old Testament: "Though he slay me, yet will I hope in him" (*NIV*). Agatha trusts, absolutely. Jesus has not saved her from death and she sees no miraculous signs of his presence. Yet she believes. She knows that through all the humiliation and agony her Lord has been with her, to support and comfort her. The comfort is not in anything she sees or hears, and it is not in anything she feels: It is in what she believes. She believes that her life is in God's hands and that her martyrdom will unite her to him.

This seems to me the essence of holiness or, if you like, the essence of our religion: We are all called to live by faith. Whatever happens to us, good or bad, we make use of it; we let it draw us to God. Agatha is praying to be rescued, and her prayer is being answered, though not in the way she would choose.

All prayer is answered, and it is answered by God in giving us grace to accept what actually happens. We can see with marvelous clarity (because Tiepolo is a great artist) what is happening to St. Agatha, the very thing she is praying to escape.

We can see too, even more marvelously, how God is enabling her to make use of her pain and her death. Her upward gaze never falters. Light shines on her physically, from the left: It shines too on the pillar and the page boy. But Tiepolo suggests another inner light, a luminescence that irradiates her interiorly. That intensity of faith brings her to heaven, while she is still most painfully on earth. This is what faith offers, here to St. Agatha, and now, today, to us.

If I had seen this painting I would not have been frightened all those years ago by St. Agatha and her breasts. Or, rather, I would have been frightened, but I would have been able, please God, to unite my fear to that of Jesus in the agony in the garden. Of course we shrink from pain and death. If Jesus did, so will we. But the death of Jesus redeemed the world, and every death, like St. Agatha's, can and should be redemptive.

St. Dorothy, died c. 300

St. Dorothy and the Infant Christ, c. 1460, Francesco di Giorgio
The National Gallery, London

St. Dorothy is not one of the more popular female saints, such as St. Mary Magdalene or St. Catherine, but the National Gallery has two very different depictions of her. The more famous is by the Master of the St. Bartholomew Altarpiece. This Dorothy is a pert, curvaceous young woman in a skintight robe of the most fetching elegance. Delightful creature though she is, I cannot warm to this reading of the saint's character.

The unknown artist who painted the small image here of St. Dorothy and the Infant Christ has never achieved more recognition than that of being associated with the better-known (yet still not a household name) Francesco di Giorgio. What it lacks in artistic skills is supplied by a touching innocence. This seems to me highly appropriate for Dorothy, who is one of the sweetest-natured among the saints.

According to legend, she refused to sacrifice to the pagan gods and was condemned to execution. As she was led through the city to her death, she passed a young lawyer called Theophilus. Apparently he was struck by her look of radiant expectation: Dorothy knew that she was on the point of seeing for herself the face of Jesus. What he saw as this foolish expression of hope infuriated Theophilus. He began to expostulate with the silly girl who, after all, could still change her mind, sprinkle the incense, and lead a normal and happy life.

Dorothy listened graciously to his contemptuous outburst, a cruel interruption on her way to paradise, and assured him that she knew what she was doing. He shouted after her that she should send him fruit and flowers when she got to heaven. He stalked off, she moved peacefully on, the executioner did his duty.

Almost immediately a small child—this artist thinks it was the Christ child, others have thought it an angel—came up to Theophilus and gave him a basket of roses and apples. Since it was winter, he had no option but to see this as a gentle response to his jeering request. We may not be surprised to learn that St. Theophilus the Lawyer himself died a martyr for the faith.

This little St. Dorothy, with her English-rose complexion and her neat waves of golden hair, her beautiful but modest garments and her air of gentle trustfulness, seems to make visual the Christian meaning of the story. A Christian is one who always treats the other with respect. Dorothy had every reason to feel hurt by the sneers of Theophilus, but she responded with a quiet humor. He asked for the impossible, fruit and flowers in winter, and she was able to prove to him that "with God all things are possible."

The little Jesus who is holding the miraculous basket looks like Dorothy's young brother. Incidentally, there are only roses in the basket—perhaps the artist was not up to painting both flowers and fruit. Dorothy holds the child Jesus with the quiet familiarity of one who has known him for many years in prayer. She looks down at her Lord with the same affectionate reverence she must have had looking up at the angry lawyer. After all, for those who love Our Lord, everyone is Our Lord. Everyone is to be treated with the love that we would offer Jesus in person. Our faith asks us to take others seriously, to listen to them, to try to help them insofar as possible. Dorothy treated Theophilus in the same way she would have wanted Christ to treat her.

Because the picture is so small it was probably painted for private devotion, the Western equivalent of the Eastern icon. I like to think of some medieval Italian family kneeling before this picture, and understanding through it the implications of Christian charity.

St. George, died c. 300

St. George and the Dragon, c. 1470, Paolo Uccello
The National Gallery, London

There seems to be historical certainty that there really was a St. George and that he was a martyr in Palestine during the persecution of Diocletian. But at some time his legend attached to itself a dragon, with a whole hinterland of drama. It was an exceptionally voracious dragon, it would seem, blackmailing a city into providing a regular meal of virgins. St. George, heroic warrior, arrived in time to save the life of the princess, who then led the dragon captive, using her girdle as a leash.

This may seem mere dramatic embellishment, but, in fact, St. George is the Christian form of a very ancient and widespread myth. Our remotest ancestors knew to the full, probably even better than we do, how threatening the world is and how helpless we are to protect ourselves. They were certainly more aware than we are of human defenselessness before winter and darkness, flood and famine. But the human heart always hopes for a hero, on a white horse, wearing armor, holding an invincible lance. When evil slithered massively forth from its darkness, the shining knight in his purity and brightness would be there to save us.

Uccello presents us with a gleaming St. George and a peculiarly repulsive dragon. In the nastiest of pretenses, this great, hideous creature sports decorative rings, as if to lull the suspicions of the powers of virtue. A nice touch is the sedate patience of the little princess, who seems quite unafraid. Not only are St. George and his horse thundering to her rescue but behind the saint's head is a strange mass of cloud, suggesting divine intervention. We can see the darkness of the gaping cave of the dragon: That will remain always sealed against the brightness of the sun. Yet what emerges from that darkness, however foul, will be overcome by the powers of goodness.

St. George then, real though he is, is not so much a person as a symbol. For the princess and her city, he is a Jesus figure. Their greatest fear and horror is the dragon against which they are helpless, and miraculously a hero comes to their rescue.

But it is a subtle symbol. Not all the work is done by the hero on his horse. He does not actually destroy the dragon, which suggests that the dragon, as a symbol of evil, is essentially indestructible. What he does is defeat the dragon, then to hand it over to that poignant symbol of frailty, the pale little princess. The saint has wounded the dragon so severely that she, representing us, can tie her girdle around its neck and lead it back to the city, harmless.

It would be more humanly satisfying a legend if we could believe that evil could be wholly removed from our lives. This story indicates that, no, dragons are a constant factor, and so are dark caves. We will not be saved without being prepared to use our girdles and walk back to the city, dragon at our heels. The Christian, who, of course, has in Jesus the supreme Savior, can never relax into complacency. Jesus will defeat our dragon whenever we ask him, but it is our dragon, and our responsibility to keep it leashed and helpless.

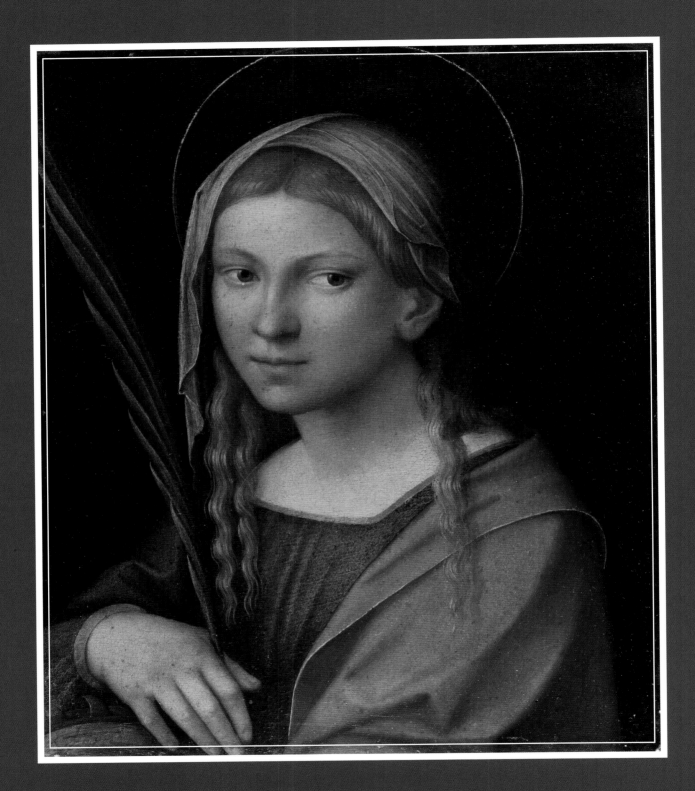

St. Catherine of Alexandria, c. 282—305

St. Catherine of Alexandria, c. 1515–1530, attributed to Benevenuto
Tisi Garofalo
The National Gallery, London

There are at least sixteen St. Catherines. All are named after the original
St. Catherine, who was one of the most popular of saints throughout
the Middle Ages and beyond. Yet, like St. Christopher, there is little
historical evidence of her existence.

There is an interesting philosophical point here: When is a saint
not a saint? The thought of St. Christopher protecting travelers has
comforted many enduring a long and perhaps dangerous journey. The
thought of St. Catherine, valiant in defense of her faith, beautiful and
wholehearted in her devotion, has inspired Christians throughout the
centuries. Artists have loved to depict both these saints. One wonders
why they were held so tenaciously in Christian memory if there was
no substratum, however small, of reality. St. Catherine is part of our
religious history and teaches us something about the nature of holiness.

One can see why some have rather balked at the melodramatics of
her legend. She was apparently a young woman of astonishing beauty,
highly born, sought in marriage by the Roman emperor himself (in some
versions the emperor's son). She refused him, citing her Christianity.

The lovelorn emperor sent fifty pagan philosophers to remonstrate
with her; Catherine converted the lot of them, whereupon the furious
emperor slaughtered the fifty new Christians, and condemned Catherine
to death upon the wheel. It was a wheel with knives attached to it (I
am not quite sure of the mechanics), and it was designed to slice its

victims to death as it turned. When Catherine was bound to the wheel, it burst free, bounded across the execution yard, and killed the wicked spectators. Gnashing his teeth, the emperor had her put to death by the infallible sword.

The wheel is the emblem in art of St. Catherine, and its appealing shape, that lovely rotundity, may be one of the reasons why artists have always been attracted to her. Raphael painted one of the most wonderful St. Catherines, all curves and amplitudes, as rounded in herself as the wheel on which she leans.

Garofalo is a relatively minor artist and this is not even positively one of his works: It is only "attributed." But I like it for its seriousness. You can just see the wheel at the bottom left corner. Catherine holds the palm branch of martyrdom and caresses it gently. The legend holds her to be a great scholar, able to argue down fifty learned pagans. There is something about this young woman, with her broad brow and widely spaced eyes, that conveys the thoughtfulness and earnestness that alone make fruitful any explanation of the faith.

It is not enough to know our religion intellectually, to be able to write articles or even books about it. What matters is to live it. We are called to a genuine relationship with Our Blessed Lord, and, in him, with the Father and the Holy Spirit. We enter this relationship at baptism and we grow in it through prayer, and the necessary sign of our prayer is goodness.

Goodness is a very wide and vague expression, yet we all know what it means. If we are not good, eager to be good, then we are not praying. If we are praying, then the inevitable result will be this practical expression of love we call goodness. I think that the legendary story of St. Catherine converting the philosophers is a dramatic expression of this. Their words came from their intellect alone; hers also came from an intellect, but a loving intellect, suffused with the grace of God.

I am also intrigued by the miracle of the wheel. We have a contemporary distaste for explosions, but it is from St. Catherine that the firework known as the Catherine wheel takes its name. It was a splendid miracle that saved her, yet what is its real significance? The wheel bursts, Catherine survives, the executioner takes a sword and finishes her. Does it not suggest strongly that earthly miracles are just that, earthly, and that we Christians have our eyes fixed on what is non-earthly and eternal?

St. Helena, c. 250–330

The Vision of St. Helena, c. 1575–1578, Paolo Veronese
The National Gallery, London

We tend to be amused and scornful about the medieval passion for relics: the slivers of the True Cross that could be rebuilt into a forest, the vial of the milk of the Virgin, the hair from the beard of John the Baptist, even a feather from the wing of the angel Gabriel. Of course, these so-called relics have utterly no religious value in themselves, yet they do represent a longing to be closer to the holy. Let us at least be willing to admit that the desire behind them is not unworthy.

The True Cross, which was so profoundly venerated in the Middle Ages and which was the focus of such genuine religious emotion, owed its existence to St. Helena. Part of the prestige of this relic came from Helena's status. She was the mother of Constantine the Great, the emperor who first removed all stigma from being Christian, and then made Christianity the Roman state religion.

Constantine, despite his religious enthusiasm, was only baptized on his deathbed, the rationale being that he could go straight from baptism to heaven. His mother, though, seems to have been a believer for some time, and she became possessed of a great desire to visit the Holy Land and worship Our Lord in the places where he suffered.

Despite her wealth and position, such a pilgrimage would have been both arduous and hazardous. When she set out, sometime after 313, she was already in her sixties, a great age for the times, though years of traveling around with her soldier husband had probably toughened her. She came into Palestine with money, influence, and great spiritual longing: We can hardly be surprised that the holy places were pointed out to her, and the "True Cross" eventually discovered.

Legend has it that while she was sleeping she had a vision of the True Cross carried by angels, and this is what Veronese shows us. His Helena is not a battered old warhorse (that was not Veronese's style), but an elegant and sensuous beauty, reclining gracefully at a window in her palace.

Having seen the cross, she was, of course, able to distinguish it from false crosses. In other words, she knew in advance that she was called to find the cross, and that she would find it—which could be a recipe for delusion. Yet is this not what we all would desire? If we were to have a vision, we think, if we were to know for certain what we were meant to do or to become, how simply and happily we could respond to God's will.

But as we know, God does not generally send us the sweet clarity of visions. We have to stumble around, praying and searching, usually quite uncertain as to whether we are doing what God wants. We envy those—and they certainly exist—who have this certainty, even when it does not come from visionary experience.

Our ignorance leaves us pitifully vulnerable. But this is precisely how we grow in closeness to Our Lord. Our ignorance forces us to recognize our need of him, and our need forces us to turn to him in prayer. He never asks for the "right decision," only the decision that, after prayer and reflection, seems to us to be right.

Looking back over the centuries, we can see that all St. Helena suffered to come close to Our Blessed Lord through his cross did bring her close to him. Whatever the truth of what she discovered, God looked at her eagerness and faith. She used the True Cross as a means of prayer, and moved through it to the Lord who hung upon it. She found him, and in him that blessed end that we all seek.

St. Jerome, c. 347–420

St. Jerome in a Rocky Landscape, c. 1520, attributed to Joachim Patinir

The National Gallery, London

For some reason, artists have always been enthusiastic about St. Jerome. He appears in two completely different settings, each of which pays tribute to one side of his complex nature. He is most famous today as a scholar, the pertinacious traveler in the Holy Land, teaching himself Hebrew, exploring Greek literature, and finally, accepting a commission to translate the entire Bible and comment on it. This life of dedicated scholarly activity intrigued artists, who loved to imagine the details of his study, with its shelves of books and all the contemporary apparatus of scholarship.

Yet St. Jerome was no dry-as-dust scholar. He was a passionate seeker after Christ, at intervals throwing aside his dictionaries and retreating into the desert to pray. There he agonized over his sinfulness, and many artists show him beating his breast with a stone or prostrate before a crucifix. Somewhere in both scenes will usually be the scarlet of a cardinal's hat, although in fact there were no cardinals in the time of Jerome. Nevertheless, he somehow seemed to artists a natural cardinal, a virtual wearer of the scarlet.

A lion is usually in the picture as well. When St. Jerome was living as a monk, he removed a thorn from a lion's paw, and the grateful beast became attached to the monastery. When thieves stole the monastic donkey, the monks blamed the lion, despite St. Jerome's passionate protests. The heartbroken animal pursued the thieves until he could bring back in triumph the missing donkey, a triumph in which St. Jerome fully shared (moral: Do not be quick to judge).

Unfortunately there is written evidence to show that St. Jerome's tenderness seems to have extended only to lions and holy women. He was a ferocious and bad-tempered correspondent, a profoundly argumentative man who could not brook disagreement. No wonder artists depict him beating his breast in contrition: He had much about which to be contrite!

Yet the passion that soured his human intellectual contacts was the same passion that was at the heart of his immense desire to love God. His years in the wilderness were precious to him, and he returned constantly either to absolute solitude or to the comparative solitude of a monastery.

This painting, typical of the artist Joachim Patinir in its sweeping bird's-eye view of the world, shows St. Jerome, small and humble, in the foreground. His companion is the faithful lion. He is clearly there to pray and to repent, possibly to repent of his bad temper and his longing for intellectual stimulation.

Intense as he was by temperament, he had times of fearing that he could not afford to enjoy literature and still give himself totally to God. The sharp and towering rocks that surround him are probably symbols of his intense and aspiring nature. Dimly in the distance can be seen the monastery and the repentant thieves, but St. Jerome has withdrawn from even the most worthy of earthly activities. Patinir suggests that the essential Jerome is not the scholar but the man of God.

St. Francis of Assisi, 1181–1226

St. Francis Renounces his Earthly Father, c. 1437–1444, Sassetta
The National Gallery, London

Francis of Assisi is everybody's favorite saint, at least to the extent that nearly everybody has heard of him and responds to him. He seems so unthreatening a saint, "Il Poverello" ("the little poor man"). He is not the only poet among the saints—St. John of the Cross is one of the greatest Spanish lyricists—but his is a poetry that is peculiarly childlike and winning.

In our environmentally conscious age, we delight in a saint who would preach to the birds and to the fish, who could persuade a rogue wolf into virtuous behavior, and who called the sun his brother and the moon his sister. Francis seems to walk happily through a world in which he sees the goodness of God on every side.

Yet to be little and poor is not merely a poetic concept. Seen in his true dimensions, no saint is more challenging than St. Francis. It is true that he was little in body, a small, dark man at whom nobody would look twice, yet whose charisma transfixed all who met him. But the littleness that he sought for himself and his order was the littleness of unimportance. He had known the pleasures of pride in his adolescence, and it was when he saw how self-importance blocked his way to the crucified Jesus that he began to thirst for "littleness" in all its aspects. The world being what it is, a sure way to unimportance is having no money and no possessions. Poverty became central to the Franciscan way of life.

Sassetta painted eight scenes from the life of St. Francis for the high altar of a Franciscan church. This one is not one of the more familiar scenes from the saint's life, but it was fundamental. He had been living at home, giving generously to the poor from his future inheritance. But the money actually, of course, still belonged to his father; and when there was domestic anger over this excessive almsgiving, St. Francis realized he must live without any security whatever. In a splendid dramatic gesture, he threw off all his clothes, and gave them back to his father. Now he possessed nothing. Symbolically, the bishop, representing the Church, threw a cloak around him.

It makes a good story, yet think of the reality of what Francis had done. From now on he would be dependent on charity. He would beg for his food; he would sleep where he could. He accepted the protection of the Church but only so that he could serve, not so that he could receive.

St. Francis was never ordained, not feeling himself worthy of the dignity of being a priest, and he held no position, even though he was the founder of a religious order. His order was to be one of "little brothers"—Friars Minor, unimportant nobodies who went around the towns and villages showing forth the joy of God. He impressed upon them that they must always be preaching, and typically he added that, if they had to, they could even use words. St. Francis and his Franciscans, that small band of unimportant men, felt called to preach by what they were.

We know that St. Francis bore the wounds of Jesus on his body, but it is more important that he had "the mind of Christ." Jesus clung to no dignity; he emptied himself. Here we see St. Francis trying to empty himself, renouncing his family, his lifestyle, and all earthly possessions present and to come.

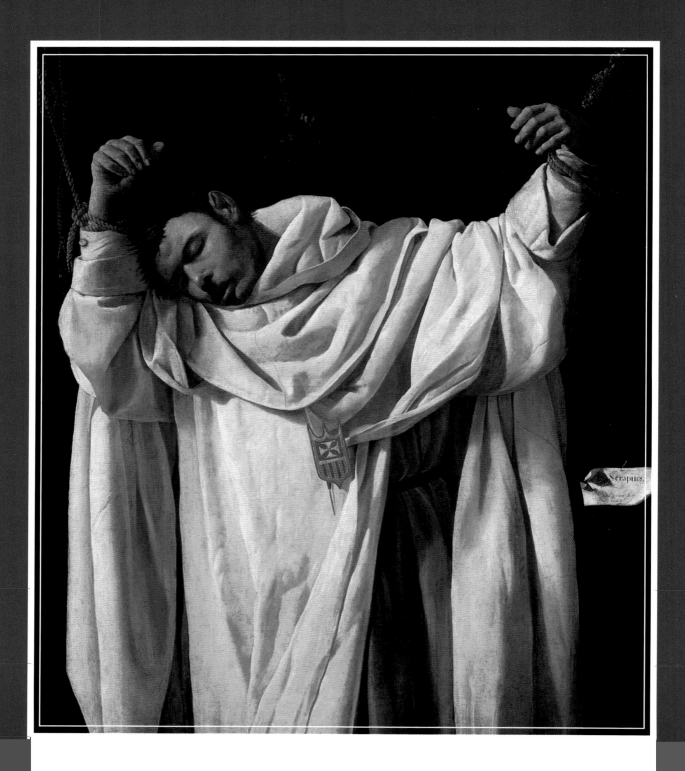

ST. SERAPION, 1178–1240

St. Serapion, 1628, Francisco de Zurbarán
Wadsworth Atheneum, Hartford, Connecticut

St. Serapion, to my surprise, turns out to have been an Englishman, Peter Serapion. He must have been both a devoted and an adventurous young man because he went to Spain to fight with the armies of Castile, as King Alfonso IX tried to hold back the Moorish invasion.

While he was there, though, Serapion was very struck by the work of the Mercedarians, a religious order that was especially established to care for those who were captured by the Muslims. Since many of these captives were tempted to buy their freedom by renouncing their faith, the Mercedarians tried to ransom them or, if that failed, to offer themselves in their place.

Serapion could see that this was the extreme expression of Christian love, giving your life for another. He joined the order in 1222, when he was already a mature soldier, and labored hard to make people understand the necessity and the greatness of this practical expression of Christian charity. I will not go into the grisly details of his death, but they included being bound hand and foot to two poles.

Zurbarán was among the greatest of artists, with a peculiarly Spanish gravitas and power. Although he was relatively young when he painted this work, he never surpassed it, nor has any other artist. It was painted for the Mercedarian monastery in Seville, to hang in the mortuary chapel where monks lay in state, awaiting their funeral

Masses. This detail is only of importance because it explains why St. Serapion is shown, as it were, asleep. His brethren, asleep in the Lord, would lie beneath this painting.

Serapion's was a gory and horrific death, and he is still hanging from the poles to which he was bound, rather as Jesus hangs from the cross. Yet—and this is the great visual glory of the painting—his thick white religious habit is spotless. It is as if, like the monks laid out in the chapel, he has been washed and reclad in full monastic dignity. Even his face, eyes closed, shows none of the trauma of his anguish.

We know little about Peter Serapion except that he gave himself to a work of charity that he thought was important, and was steadfast to death. But those great swags of thick white cloth, on which light and shade both play, suggest the underlying purity of such a life. He gave himself to love; love cleanses and sanctifies him. The garment seems symbolic of the man. A vocation truly understood and embraced bears us up within itself.

Few of us will be called to lead a life dedicated to so heroic a purpose as that of the Mercedarians. Thank God we no longer need an order whose members will sell themselves into slavery to ransom others!

But to some extent being a mercedarian, with a small *m,* is part of the Christian faith. Jesus repeated, again and again, how essential it is that we should serve one another, that our love should be self-sacrificing and practical.

For some people every day offers opportunities for many mini-martyrdoms: small surrenders of their own freedom for the sake of others. These sacrifices have no apparent grandeur about them, and we know that, in actuality, St. Serapion's sacrifice would have been the absolute opposite of grand or sublime. It would have been horrible, completely without dignity, dirty and bloody.

Zurbarán shows us not the facts but the truth, and, in the calm amplitude in which the dying saint stretches out his arms in death, we have an image of that sacrificial surrender that Our Lord asks of us in our ordinary lives. Zurbarán makes it clear that this is not meant to be a literal painting, by imitating, on the right side, a label with his signature.

The whites and the blacks, the light and the dark, the monumental stillness of this work are all an implicit celebration of sacrificial holiness.

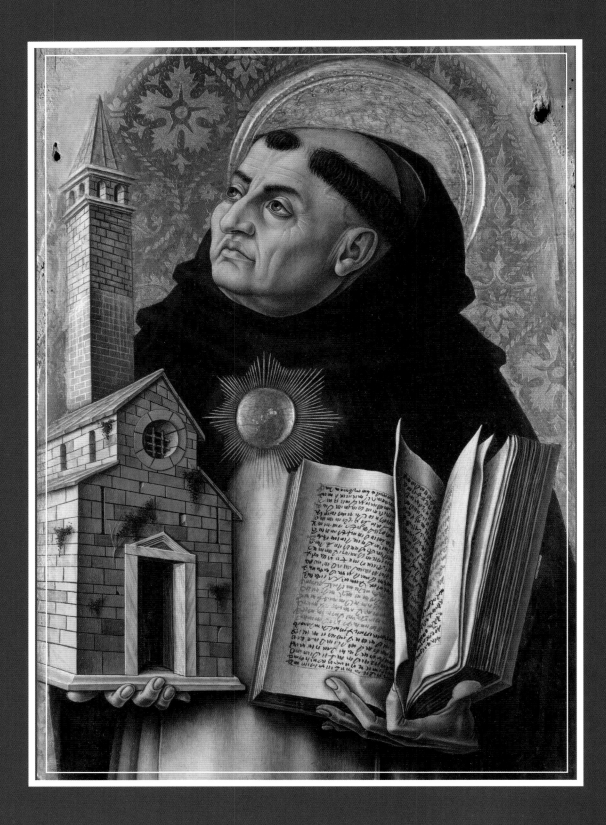

St. Thomas Aquinas, 1225–1274

St. Thomas Aquinas, 1476, Carlo Crivelli
The National Gallery, London

There seem to have been quite a few clever saints (St. Augustine, St. Teresa of Avila) and the occasional genius (St. Francis and, to my mind, St. Thérèse of Lisieux). But St. Thomas Aquinas is in a class of his own. Intellectually, he dominated the Middle Ages, the great "angelic doctor"—*doctor*, remember, meaning "teacher." He taught the Church in his own day, and he teaches it still.

Aquinas's *Summa Theologica* may no longer be the only source of the Church's theology, but it remains an extraordinary achievement and will always reward study. Crivelli shows St. Thomas holding his teaching in one hand, while in the other he clasps to himself the beloved Church. Between the book and the Church we can see the outlines of a star: He was an essential light-bringer.

What St. Thomas did for the Church, with the finesse, clarity, and authority that no theologian has ever equaled, was to bring order to the complexities of religious speculation. He drew out the meaning of the Gospels and of St. Paul, while simultaneously exploring the powerful and often daunting rationality of Aristotle. He showed how faith could not but be both in accord with reason and above it, though never at odds with it. One is still awed by the vastness of his mental capacity, and the simplicity with which he could strip the most abstruse doctrine down to its fundamentals, analyze it, and show its relationship to the whole body of faith.

Artists tend to show this great scholar as an ascetic figure, worn out by his constant nightly vigils. Crivelli has the truth of it, or rather, is more truthful than most. His Thomas is a burly figure with a large, good-humored face. The real Thomas was immensely fat. This may well have been the result of a metabolic disorder, yet in this age of obesity it is a comfort to think that at least one saint experienced for himself the painful burden of too much flesh. Poor St. Thomas actually had to have a semicircle cut out of the table in the friars' refectory so that he could get within touching distance of the meager Dominican fare.

He joined the Dominicans against parental opposition. His family was aristocratic, and wanted him to be a lordly Benedictine abbot. Highborn or not, he was, apparently, a large, shambling, shy young man with a ready smile and slow speech. The other novices called him "the dumb ox," and his teacher, St. Albert, another great Dominican scholar, told them in reproof that the bellowings of this dumb ox would enlighten the world. Despite his unromantic appearance, Thomas was a true poet. The "O Salutaris Hostia" and the "Tantum Ergo," which we sing in honor of the Blessed Sacrament, were written by St. Thomas.

Faith will tell us Christ is present,
when our human senses fail.

—"Tantum Ergo"

His faith was intense. At the end of his life, though he was still a youngish man, in his forties, he said that he could write about God no more. All he had written, he said, "seemed like straw."

St. Bernadette, 1844–1879

Bernadette's Embroidery, 2008, Greg Tricker
Piano Nobile Gallery, London

One of the abiding fascinations of St. Bernadette is that there is so little to get hold of. It baffled her superiors in the convent, and it baffles us today. She was in the paradoxical position of receiving the sustained and admiring attention of millions, while feeling herself to be of the utmost insignificance.

In some ways, hers was a peculiarly passive life. It was not what she did but what was done to her, for her, that was of such universal significance. We all know the story of Lourdes, and how this little peasant girl, poor, malnourished (she was fourteen but looked about eleven), sickly, uneducated, was visited one spring morning by Our Blessed Lady. This astonishing event marked her forever as different.

Remember, the crowds who flocked to Lourdes to see Bernadette talking to the lady saw nothing but Bernadette herself. There was nothing whatever to prove that this was not a gigantic hallucination: no gentle breezes, no glimmering light, nothing. Yet Bernadette was herself her own authentication. The crowds looked at this little creature, with her face upturned toward what she alone could see, and even the most cynical or skeptical were silenced. The visions came to an end, but what they had started never ended.

Bernadette could not see that this was anything to do with her. She gave as an example taking a broom from behind the door, sweeping with it, and then back behind the door it goes again. She saw herself as that broom: Our Lady had used her and put her away, and there was no credit owing to Bernadette herself.

She suffered intensely from the continuing interest of pilgrims, putting up patiently but with inner rebellion, with their intrusive questioning and the sound of their cameras. She desired with all her heart that what Our Lady wanted would come about: that there would be a church built in her honor and that people would pray the rosary. But having told the authorities, which for her meant her parish priest, she felt that it was now in safe hands. She treasured in her heart what had happened: She had no desire to speak about it, she had no desire to be noticed.

It is Bernadette's life as a nun that most attracts me, especially since one feels that she only became a nun because it seemed the best thing to do. It protected her privacy. The nuns were both deeply impressed to have the visionary come among them and, even more deeply, taken aback by how ordinary she was. She was a person no one would notice.

Greg Tricker has noticed her, has understood with his own unique sensitivity the humble innocence of this young woman. He has sculpted, painted, drawn, and etched images that show all the aspects of her life. *Bernadette's Embroidery* shows her nearing the end. What we see here is the seriousness of her concentration: She can no longer work for the community, so she does what she can do to the best of her ability.

The artist has touched her with blue to suggest the constancy with which she thought of Mary. This is a painting of prayer, of that simple, absolute surrender to God that gives God freedom to act.

It is painful to read about Bernadette's life in the convent and its harshness. She accepted it all quietly, often subduing her robust peasant spirit so as to accept humbly and gratefully whatever happened. Her death was long and painful, but she clung to the Hail Mary in her heart, with total trust and submission. "Pray for us sinners, now and at the hour of our death." "Us sinners, us sinners" were her last words, because nobody is more aware than a saint of our profound need of God's forgiveness.

St. Thérèse of Lisieux, 1873–1897

Photograph, 1881

Carmelite Monastery, Lisieux, France

Although there are many pictures of saints, few are actually portraits. Those saints who did have their portraits painted were mostly unfortunate in not attracting artists of much skill. The only exception that comes to mind is St. Thomas More, who was painted by Holbein, though it was his position as statesman and celebrated intellectual that was being recorded, not so much his sanctity.

Thérèse of Lisieux was painted quite often, mostly by her sister and fellow Carmelite, Céline. But these works, however deep the love that prompted them, are hardly art.

Fortunately, Céline also took many photographs, and here we are in the unusual position of knowing in hard actuality what St. Thérèse looked like. All agree that she was angelically pretty, an opinion not wholly borne out by the photographs. She is pretty, of course, with her big blue eyes and cascades of hair, but she has an overlong and very determined chin. It is the chin, rather than the curls, that gives us an insight into Thérèse. When we consider that she died when she was twenty-four, it seems to me that she was as much a genius, spiritually, as was Mozart or Shakespeare artistically.

The photograph I have chosen is not one of those Céline took inside the monastery. This one was taken by a professional photographer when Thérèse was eight. Her mother had died four years earlier, and Thérèse was now the adored youngest of a family of six sisters. Both parents were devout Catholics, and all the girls became nuns, five of them Carmelites in Lisieux.

Here we see Thérèse, dressed to the nines, ruffled and flounced, her hair an elaborate arrangement of ringlets. Her father, Louis Martin, assuaged his grief over his wife's death by enshrining in his affections his "little queen." She was spoiled and pampered, not an easy child but one surrounded by constant love and admiration. She acknowledges herself how self-willed she was, and who could wonder at it?

When her two eldest sisters, Marie and Pauline, became Carmelites, fifteen-year-old Thérèse determined to follow them, despite clerical opposition. Her steely insistence brought her what she desired. This is hardly the recipe for a life of supreme holiness, yet Thérèse turned all its disadvantages—her privileged upbringing, her special status as community darling—into positive assets. All we need to become close to God is to desire it and to let God achieve it within us. This young teenager desired God with a passion that cut through all pretense.

The culture of her milieu made very much of physical penance: Thérèse, who so longed to be a saint, saw that the sisters most admired in the monastery were those who undertook the most severe penance. Here is where we see her genius. She could cut through all the romanticism and look straight to God. The Jesus we see in the Gospels was uninterested in physical mortification. He never suggested that his followers should scourge themselves, and his attitude toward fasting raised not a few contemporary eyebrows. The life of Carmel was hard enough in itself. Thérèse saw that it was not necessary to look for suffering: The suffering was there for everybody, just in the daily course of living.

God did not ask for extraordinary deeds; God asked for love. Thérèse, instructed only by her own prayer, set herself on what she called her "Little Way." This meant that she did everything for love, even the smallest things, like picking up a pin, smiling when she felt irritated, listening patiently to the boring tales of other sisters, not defending herself when her actions were misinterpreted. It sounds simple, and it is simple, but it is very far from easy. To lead a life wholly given to loving God in the small actualities of every day means a complete surrender of all selfishness and pride.

I have always been very moved by what she said about God's mercy. Everybody prays for mercy: Thérèse said that she expected as much from God's justice as from God's mercy. This was not at all because she felt that she was blameless—far from it. What she did feel was that blame, as well as praise, was God's business.

Thérèse sought truth and she grasped, as very few have done, that it is only God who knows the complete truth. Neither family nor the closest of friends, nor we ourselves, really know the full truth of what we are and what we can be. The whole range of our weakness and of our strengths, the full weight of early experience and what it has made of us—all these factors are known only to God. Of all the saints, I feel St. Thérèse teaches us most surely about what it is to love.